What Leaders are saying about this book...

In a leadership role? Don't know what to do? Read this book! NOW!!! It contains very many useful ideas for those in a leadership role and invaluable lessons for leaders who appreciate the value of execution; and it does this in a compact, easy to read format.

- Ed Minich,
President & CEO,
Otis Canada

As an entrepreneur, the book taught me so much! It inspired me to be a better leader and reinforced the notion of how important teamwork is to success. It describes vividly the passion and courage it takes to run a company and manage people. And it shows that, in business, it is vital to never give up. But, perhaps more than anything else, Bart's book helped me realize that a mission statement can be an important marketing tool. I think this book is an excellent template for anyone interested in implementing their mission and wanting to make it come alive. *It's what everyone who develops a mission statement needs to know!*

- Ron Foxcroft,
President and Founder,
The Fox 40 Whistles   *more...*

Bart's book speaks to the reality that you have to make tough personal choices in business. I particularly liked the way he set out the stages of discovery. They are put into an engaging format so that the reader has an emotional attachment to the outcome and therefore a buy-in to the message of the book. There are many nice gems in here and the book carries a powerful message for aspiring leaders.

- John Grant
Managing Director, Investment Banking
RBC Capital Markets

As a CEO, I know my number one challenge: "getting others to understand and execute our strategy". In an interesting and easy read, Bart provides a "step by step" guide to company leadership. A guide to which I now frequently refer and one that can help my entire management team get the most out of our employees.

- Gerry Smith,
CEO,
Changepoint Corporation

still more...

Excellent, easy/quick to read and remember...*and practical.* You don't want to stop reading till you finish. Highly recommended reading for all - at school, university, home or office.

- Harry Govind,
Assistant Director, Information Management, IATA

A great working manual for State Farm to help our agents – both trainees and established ones - understand clearly 'what', 'why' and 'how'...or they just don't get it. And a clear understanding for management to make sure that we deliver on our leadership training. I am sure this will be a great seller.

- Bill Karda, **Agency Field Executive**
State Farm Insurance

keep going...

A feature that I thought was very good, was the fact that Bart did not leave basic and obvious details for the reader to assume. He placed them in the book which I think is good for young and potential managers. I have read the "One Minute Manager" and "Who moved my cheese?". I can safely say this book compliments them.

- Resic Hansen,
Manager, Technical Operations Centre,
Air Jamaica

It's an easy read...and when I read it the second time, the more impressed I became. Bart has, in a very short span, outlined, not only the mission, its why's, how's and implementation, but gathered the fundamentals of leadership, culture, human resource management and business philosophy. While basic, the book gives the reader a short thesis of the interplay between all of these areas in modern business. A great job. This book works well for business students at all levels, for supervisors, managers and those who aspire to become them. My congratulations to the author.

- Brian E. Jones,
Vice President, Finance & Administration
Wilton Industries Canada Ltd.

A
Tale
of
Two Employees

& the person who wanted to lead them.

by
Dr. Chris Bart, F.C.A.

"Simple truths for getting almost anyone to do what needs to be done"

For Tom, it was the best of times and it was the worst of times. It was the best of times because he had just been promoted to a new job - a position that he had wanted and worked for very hard. The job meant more pay, more status, more authority and, of course, more responsibility. And Tom, who was regarded as a clever young man, liked all of that.

But it was also the worst of times, because after just a few weeks in his new position, Tom worried that he was not going to succeed; that he was going to FAIL!

And why?

Because the two employees that reported to him, Rick and Harry, were for some reason *not doing what the company needed them to do*.

You see, Tom's job had many different aspects. The majority of his work involved gathering, analyzing and interpreting data and then reporting the results to others. This took about 90 percent of Tom's time and he did this very well. In fact, he had already received some positive feedback from his superiors telling him how good his reports were and how well he personally appeared to be adapting to his new responsibilities.

The rest of Tom's job, however, involved managing two front-line workers, Rick and Harry. Their job was to answer the company's main telephone line, direct calls to other company members and occasionally take customer orders over the phone. They were also responsible for checking weekly company 'time sheets' for completeness and accuracy as well as receiving and organizing the shipment of all courier and express post packages and envelopes. According to Tom, this should have been a relatively easy job to perform. "After all," he thought many times to himself, *"this isn't rocket science!"* And yet, based on the information that he had just received from a recently instituted customer satisfaction report, both Rick and Harry were not meeting company or customer "expectations".

Those expectations were embodied in the ***company's new mission statement***. It was posted on every wall and on the back of every business card. The company even had T-shirts made with the mission printed on it and gave one to every employee.

The new mission was announced with a flourish of fanfare and inspiring speeches. Everyone was told to ***embrace*** the mission, to ***live*** the mission ***and to make it their own***. It read:

Our mission
is to provide products of
the highest level
of quality and service
that will truly delight and amaze
each and every customer
we are privileged to serve.

We are committed
to providing our employees
with opportunities for learning
and personal growth.
Above all,
employees will be provided
the same respect, appreciation and
caring attitude
that they are expected
to give each customer.

We will recognize
achievement
and be socially responsible
members
of the community.

After the mission was introduced, everyone was asked to sign a huge poster on which the mission was printed thereby signifying each person's acceptance and support of it. Everyone signed it - including Tom, Rick and Harry.

The customer satisfaction report that Tom received, however, stated that customers were "DISSATISFIED" with their experience when telephoning the company. They said their experience was not one of "delight" or "amazement".

"Why won't they do what the company needs them to do?" Tom asked himself. "They were present for the launch of the new mission four weeks ago. They even signed the mission declaration. Why are they holding back and resisting?"

Tom was unsure what to do. Since this was the first time that he had to manage others, he did not want to make any mistakes. He knew that, even though his managerial responsibilities constituted only a small percentage of his total job, they held the key to future promotions and success with the company. And so he knew that if he got off on the wrong foot with his two subordinates, they could jeopardize his career. And Tom liked the career path that he thought he was on.

Because he was a clever young man, Tom decided to consult his mentor, Fred - a wise old man who had been with the company for many, many years. Everyone respected Fred because Fred always got the job done. According to Tom's informal sources, Fred was already seen as the person who was excelling at driving home the new mission in his department.

"I should talk with Fred", thought Tom. And so he called the wise old man to arrange a convenient time to chat.

Fred told Tom to come by immediately.

The First Question

When Tom arrived at Fred's office, he was greeted warmly by the wise old man. Fred liked Tom. He knew that Tom was a clever young man and that he could have a great career with the company. It made Fred happy to think that he might play a role in helping to make that happen.

"So", asked Fred "what's the problem that you need to see me about? I would have thought that you didn't need any more advice from an old man like me. But, I'm always glad to see you and happy to help in any way that I can."

"Thanks, Fred", replied Tom. "But, you taught me long ago that it is never wrong to seek out anyone's opinion when you have a problem that you're not sure how to solve. As a matter of fact, you impressed upon me the view that a person should get as many opinions from as many wise old men like yourself when faced with a difficult problem."

Fred laughed. "Okay," he said "you've learned your lessons from me very well. But, enough of the flattery young man. What can I do for you?"

Tom explained his managerial dilemma: "I have two workers reporting to me who are responsible for answering the company's main telephone lines. They answer the phone, redirect callers and sometimes take orders. They also have some other clerical duties. But they are not living the company's new mission in their job. The first customer satisfaction report that I've received says that our customers are not at all satisfied with their telephone experience."

"I see," said Fred. Then, after a few seconds of silence he asked, "But, *do they know what to do?*"

"Do they know what to do?" a perplexed Tom repeated back aloud. "Well, they should!" he exclaimed excitedly. "Both Rick and Harry were present when the new mission was unveiled. They both heard the speeches. They both signed the poster. I've even seen Rick wearing the new T-shirt with the mission printed on it. There is also a plaque containing the company's mission right behind their desks that they would see every day when they come into work. So, I would say that they both know what to do."

Fred, who was watching Tom's animated response closely, replied quietly "Yes, Tom, I hear what you are saying, but let me ask you again: Do Rick and Harry really *know what to do*?"

"I'm not quite sure I understand what you mean." Tom asked haltingly.

"Well then, let me try to be more clear." replied Fred. "Do Rick and Harry know the new mission?"

"Know the new mission? Of course they know it", replied Tom, somewhat peeved with Fred's persistent question. "How could they not know it given all that we have done to communicate it to them?"

"You' re right", Fred replied. "They should know it. But, before we continue, why don't you go and check this out for yourself, just to be sure. Besides, I really have to get back to my own work right now since my boss needs to see me in about 45 minutes. Come back and see me tomorrow when you've had a chance to find out the answer to my question. Okay?"

"Alright," said Tom. And with that, the two men shook hands. Tom then returned to his work area where Rick and Harry were stationed. It was late in the day, almost quitting time. Tom decided to act while the conversation with the wise old man was still fresh in his head.

He called his two workers aside. "Rick, Harry…" he began, " I know this might seem like a dumb question, but, uh…you both know about the current mission…right?"

"Oh, sure we do" chimed Harry. "We all remember the big party that we had a few weeks back to introduce it. It was a lot of fun."

"The bosses gave some pretty good speeches" echoed Rick "some of the better ones that they've ever made, I might add. My wife also really liked the T-shirt. Said it was made of a high-quality cotton."

Tom steeled himself as he prepared for his next words. "I'm glad you remember that we got a new mission statement awhile back. But, do you remember what the mission statement said exactly? Do either of you remember any of the words in it?" He held his breath.

"Well, uh, not really." Said Rick.

"Didn't it pretty well say much of the same old stuff …..something about the customer?" asked Harry. "Not much new in my opinion!"

"Fred was right," thought Tom as he bowed his head in despair. "They don't know the mission. They don't *know what to do*." At that, he said "Thanks guys. Let's call it a day."

On the car-ride home that night, Tom reflected on his conversation with Fred and what had happened with Rick and Harry.

The next day, Tom phoned his mentor Fred and arranged a time to resume their discussion. As Tom entered Fred's office, the wise old man boomed: "So, my clever young man, how did it go with Rick and Harry?"

"Just as you suspected", a dejected Tom answered. "They don't *know what to do* because they don't know the mission. But that surprises me after everything the company has done to make sure that we all know about the new mission."

"Does it really?" replied Fred. "Did you really think that once all the hoopla died down about the new mission that it would have any impact or relevance? Oh sure, the company did a fine job *acquainting* everyone with the mission and *informing* us that there was a new one. They did all the usual stuff. And the company should be commended for this because some organizations expect their employees to be mind-readers when it comes to knowing their important messages...

"But, what they did could hardly be called *effective communication*. In fact, it's been my experience that just because someone has an important message, like the mission, to send out to the rest of the organization, and it has been *sent*, it doesn't always necessarily follow that the message will automatically be heard or *received*, let alone *remembered* by the sender's intended audience. And, when you think about it, *if people have not heard a message, especially an important one such as the company's mission, they can't even begin to live it and they won't* ***know what to do***. Now for a message to be received and remembered, you have to take a few extra steps."

"Like what" asked Tom.

"Like ***relentlessly repeating*** the mission!" exclaimed Fred. "You have to ***recite it and repeat it over and over again*** so that no one forgets it. And you have to refer to it all the time. It's not just enough to have the mission printed on plaques, business cards and T-shirts. You found that out for yourself with Rick and Harry. Instead, you have to imprint the mission, or any other important message, onto your brain if it's going to have any impact."

"Interesting" Tom interjected. "And how exactly do you go about doing that?"

"Well" the wise old man replied "we do a lot of things."

"Such as…?"

"To begin with," said Fred, "I told everyone on my staff - about 20 people - that I expected them to memorize the new mission. I also told them that I would approach each of them on a random basis and ask them to recite it on the spot. If they could recite it, I would buy them a coffee. If they couldn't, then I would try to recite the mission and if I could, then they would have to buy me a coffee. And if I couldn't, I would still have to buy them the coffee. Sometimes, I made the bet for lunch or some other reward…such as washing their car on my lunch break."

"But you also mentioned that you refer to it a lot. How do you do that?" asked Tom.

"That's a bit harder….because you always have to be vigilant for opportunities to do so…take birthday celebrations, for instance. We used to have little informal parties for my staff simply because we liked doing it. Today, though, I always make a point of remarking to the team that the reason why we have these parties is because it's just another one of the small ways in which we try to show the *'appreciation and caring attitude'* embodied in our mission. Taking this approach, we can connect our specific actions to the mission and people can see that the words are not fake...that the words are real....

"But, now, let me ask you this," Fred continued. "And please forgive me for being cruel when I say this...but, Tom, do you know the mission?... Can you tell me what it says?"

"What do you mean?" stammered the clever young man.

"I mean", Fred replied "Can you recite the mission for me?"

"You want me to recite the mission for you, here?.....Right now?"

"Yes" replied Fred with a hint of sarcasm in his voice. "Recite the company's mission for me... if you can."

Tom began slowly: "The mission of our company is...is.......is to .....to provide ......high quality service....to all of our customers…. all the time. Or something very close to that……right?"

"Not really." said Fred and he then recited the mission perfectly for Tom.

"Tom," he continued, " I'm really quite disappointed in your answer because the first thing that good leaders learn is *never to ask a subordinate to do anything that they are not prepared to do themselves if they have to*. **A good leader leads by example**. How can you expect Rick and Harry to take the mission seriously when you yourself aren't even doing so?"

"You're right", said Tom as he made a mental note to himself to learn the mission *by heart* that afternoon.

"But, is there anything else that I can do to help my employees remember the mission?" Tom inquired.

"Oh sure." Fred replied. "For instance, we usually begin our weekly staff meeting with everyone reciting the mission en masse. We have even begun having occasional 'mission quizzes' in which we give everyone a copy of the mission with key words deleted and then ask each person to individually fill in the blanks. We then post the ranked results on the department bulletin board for everyone to see."

Fred then reached into his desk drawer and pulled out a sheet of paper.

He handed it to Tom.

On the page was the company's mission written as follows:

The Mission Quiz

Our mission

is to provide -------- of

the ------- level

of ------- and -------

that will ----- ------- and -----

---- and every --------

we are ---------- to -----.

We are ---------

to providing our ---------

with opportunities for --------

and -------- ------.

Above all,

employees will be --------

with the same -------, ------------

and --------- attitude

that they are --------

to give each --------.

We will recognize -----------

and be -------- ----------- members

of the ---------.

"And this works?" Tom asked.

"Let's go see for yourself" the wise old man answered and at that, he got up, motioned for Tom to follow him and walked out into his department's work area. The first desk they stopped at was Fred's secretary, Betty.

"Betty," said Fred, "this is Tom and I've been telling him all about our efforts to learn the company's new mission. Can you recite it for him?" Betty smiled and with absolutely no effort, the words of the company mission statement rolled off her lips. Fred then had Tom randomly select three other employees from the work area to approach and ask to recite the mission. Each sailed through the request. Tom was impressed and vowed to himself that, someday soon, Rick and Harry would be able to do the same. "They, too, will *know what to do*," he thought.

Tom then thanked the wise old man for his time and professed his eagerness in getting back to his own department so that he could begin putting into practice some of the ideas that he had learned. Fred told him to come back anytime if the clever young man had any more concerns.

Over the next several weeks, Tom worked diligently at making sure that both Rick and Harry knew the mission. He told them that he expected them to memorize it. Rick, however, complained that he thought the mission was too hard to memorize because it was "much too long!" Tom was prepared for this, though, and when he recited the mission for both employees, Rick's jaw dropped.

"You must have a good memory", exclaimed Rick. "I could never do that."

"Actually, Rick, I have a lousy memory", Tom replied. "But, I thought about some of the stuff that I've memorized in the past. The pledge of allegiance, for instance. Some prayers. And even the words to a favorite song. I suddenly realized that the only way that I learned them *by heart* was by first, committing to learn them and second, by **relentlessly repeating the words, over and over again** until I had it right. That's all there is to memorizing anything. I did it and so can you".

Tom then promised that he would help both employees memorize the mission. In fact, he challenged them to a free coffee the next day if they both could recite it. Tom was only half disappointed. Rick came in with the mission well memorized. Harry, on the other hand, said that he forgot all about it. He promised, though, to have it memorized by lunch but, then, stumbled through it. Rick told Harry that he expected him to do better. Harry promised that he would "know it cold" and "have it nailed" the next day - which, he did.

Thereafter, Tom made it a regular practice to have "mission drills" and he even "borrowed" the wise old man's mission quiz and used it, as a bet, to see who would have to go and fetch lunch for the three of them.

Time passed and Tom, being a clever young man, grew increasingly confident of both employees' ability to know the mission. "They now *know what to do*" said Tom - a bit smugly - to himself. "The message has been sent. The message has been received. And the message has been remembered. Fred would be very proud of me."

Imagine Tom's surprise, then, when after several more weeks, the next customer satisfaction report was issued and, based on the statistics, it indicated that there was virtually no change in the ratings for Tom's department. Customers were still reporting being "DISSATISFIED" with the quality and level of service being received when telephoning the company.

"This is not possible", cried Tom. "Rick and Harry both know the mission." To confirm this, he jumped up from behind his desk and walked over to the doorway where he spotted Harry. "Quick, Harry," he said, "what's the company's mission?"

"That's easy" Harry replied and he rhymed off the sentences flawlessly. Then Harry added, "How did I do, boss?"

"Great Harry, just great." responded Tom, but without the usual enthusiasm in his voice.

"What's wrong?"

"I'm not sure", answered Tom as he quickly darted towards the elevator.

A few moments later, Tom was standing outside Fred's office. The door was ajar and Fred was just hanging up his telephone.

Tom stuck his head inside the office and asked with just a tinge of anxiousness in his voice, "Got a moment, Fred?"

Fred could see that Tom was somewhat upset, so he said: "Sure Tom, but I've only got about five minutes. Is it urgent?"

"Sort of…" Tom said. "You remember our previous conversation about my two employees that I was concerned about…Rick and Harry? Well, I've just gotten my department's latest customer satisfaction report and the results indicate that customers are still not happy with their experience when telephoning into the company. So, I don't understand what's going on Fred? How do you explain this?"

"*Do they know what to do?*" the wise old man asked.

"Do they know what to do?" repeated Tom almost shouting. "Of course, they know what to do. I have done everything that we talked about the last time. I have told them that I needed them to memorize the mission. And they have done it. We recite it all of the time. Harry even just did it for me moments before I came to see you. So, they know the mission…The message has been sent. The message has been received. The message is remembered…But they still aren't doing what the company needs them to do."

"I see," said Fred. "But let me try something with you, Tom. I am going to say some words for you. Okay? Here they are: 'dog', 'cat', flower', 'tree'.

"Dog, cat, flower, tree?" repeated Tom quizzically.

"That's right", the wise old man responded. "Dog, cat, flower, tree. When I say those words, tell me what is happening inside your brain. If I am not mistaken, you actually see a picture of a cat or dog or flower or tree."

"You're right", Tom said.

Fred continued: "We think best when we think in pictures…when we can 'see' what is being said. Now, let me say some other words for you, Tom. 'Highest quality', 'highest service', 'truly delight and amaze'. Tell me what you 'see' when I say some of the key words from our company's new mission to you?"

"Nothing" responded Tom. "I see nothing. Just fog."

"And if <u>YOU</u> only see fog when I say those words, Tom, then just imagine what Rick and Harry see. "

"Probably the same thing," Tom replied weakly.

"Absolutely", boomed Fred. "So when I asked you *'Do they know what to do?'* the real answer should have been 'No, they don't'. Yes, the *mission message has been sent, received and remembered*. But it still has not been *understood* to the point where Rick and Harry can 'see' what the words actually mean. As a matter of fact Tom, I also have to confess a bit of a bias when it comes to saying things a certain way. I actually prefer and value the phrase *"I see"* more than the phrase "I understand" because you can 'understand' the need for customer satisfaction and yet, still not 'see' what it entails or what it involves....And so, only when someone can 'see' what it is that they are supposed to do will they really be able to say that they *know what to do*."

"I think I'm beginning to understand….er, I mean, I SEE", Tom chuckled. "But how can I get them to 'see' the mission message?"

"Now, Tom, that's part of what being a leader is all about" responded Fred with a hint of impatience growing in his voice. *__Leaders help others translate the words in the mission message so that they have meaning for them__. So that others can say 'I see'."

"And do you have any advice on how I should go about doing this?" Tom asked.

"Sure Tom, there are many things that you could do. But, my time with you is running out… so why don't you come back and see me tomorrow about 11:30 am." And at that, Fred flew out the door leaving Tom to ponder everything that the wise old man had said.

As he walked back towards his office, Tom jotted some notes on the pad of paper that he was carrying:

Tom's Notes...

In order for employees *to know what to do*, a leader must *communicate effectively* with them. A leader should make sure that:

- The message containing what employees are expected to do is *sent* (employees are not mind readers). This is one of the purposes of mission.
- The message is *received*. Just because a message is sent does not mean that it has been heard. Test for active listening.
- The message is *understood*. The message should be clear and have meaning so that employees can say 'I see'. *Leaders help others to translate the words.*
- The message is *remembered*. Relentlessly repeating over and over again important messages helps to keep them current and alive. A message not remembered is the same as a message not sent. *Leaders lead by example.*

IF the message is not sent, received, understood or remembered, employees WILL NOT KNOW WHAT TO DO!

The next day, Tom returned to Fred's office to pick up where they had left off. "You were about to explain how I might help Rick and Harry better **understand** the mission message so that they will **know what to do**." Tom began.

"That's right," the wise old man replied "and there are many things that you might do. But, let me turn your question back on you. *How do you think you might* go about helping Rick and Harry translate the mission message so that it has meaning for them...so that they will **know what to do** when it comes to living the mission? What are some of the things that you could do to help them?" Fred then grabbed for a pad of paper on his desk and handed it to Tom.

"Here", he said. "*Write down all of the things that you might possibly do to answer this question*...and DON'T pre-judge your ideas. Just write them down as quickly as possible."

After about two minutes, Tom handed back to the wise old man the page with his answers on it. It read:

Tom's List

1. Tell Rick and Harry what I think the mission words mean and tell them what I specifically want them to do.

2. Do a customer survey to find out what customers expect given the words in the mission and then inform Rick and Harry.

3. Ask Rick and Harry what they think the words in the mission mean.

4. Do all of the above.

"That's a great list" smiled Fred. "Now, which one should you do?

"The one that I want to do is to simply tell Rick and Harry what to do" replied Tom.

"Why?" inquired the wise old man.

"Because, that's what a leader does, right? I have to let them know who is in charge so that they will know that I am the boss. Besides, it's also the quickest solution. "

"It may be quick" replied Fred "but it can also be extremely costly....the reason being that taking your approach presumes that you are right...that you have the correct answer....which, of course, you may not...and if you don't, you'll look like an idiot in the eyes of Rick and Harry.... Yet, don't get me wrong, Tom, you should still make sure that you have your own ideas about how the words translate as well."

"So, then, if I read you right," interjected Tom, "I should probably first try to do a customer survey to find out what our customers want and how they would interpret the words in our mission. Only then will I really know the correct meaning of the words."

"You could, you should and you must do that. The customer's perspective is vital. But there are several things that you need to bear in mind as you do the survey. The first is that the customer may not know what he or she wants…or may not be able to express it. The other problem that might emerge is that it may take some time organizing the survey or focus group, collecting the data and interpreting the results. And, it will, for sure, if you ask our customer relations department to organize it for you. In the meantime, you can expect your customers to still be "DISSATISFIED" with their experience when telephoning into the company. So, my advice to you is to, at least, try to do it yourself while you wait for their report confirming – or denying - what you have found. "

"I see" said Tom. "So, are you saying that the "correct answer" is number three?"

Fred laughed. "I'm not *telling* you anything, Tom. I'm just **helping** you and me arrive at a preferred alternative. Now, think about it. What are some of the advantages from asking Rick and Harry for their thoughts?"

"To begin with" said Tom "I get to hear their ideas and see if they have any that might be better than mine."

"Absolutely!" roared Fred. "But there's another advantage which is probably just as important."

"And what's that?" inquired Tom.

"It's how Rick or Harry will feel if you adopt any of their suggestions or proposed solutions and then give them credit for it. How do you think that it would make them feel, Tom?"

"I would guess pretty good," replied Tom.

"Not just pretty good, Tom, but GREAT!" bellowed Fred "and why? Because they want what everyone wants: *to feel good about themselves, to feel important, to feel that their opinion counts and that what they do here matters*. In other words, *everyone wants to feel respected, valued, and appreciated*. That's why we say what we do in our mission. Tom…you know, the part that goes: 'Above all, employees will be provided the same respect, appreciation and caring attitude that they are expected to give each customer.' We believe that everyone wants this and, from what I have read, all the research on employee satisfaction tends to support this."

"I see," said Tom.

"And so, Tom, one of the possible ways we might try to satisfy this need that all employees feel" Fred continued, "is *by asking them questions* …by asking for their ideas and opinions…and by acknowledging and thanking them for their contributions. When I do this, my people know that *I need them and that I depend on them for getting things done. They feel 'worth-full', not worthless.*"

"But what if they give you a dumb answer? Or, one that you think is incorrect or stupid?…Then what do you do?"

"Now, let me turn the question back on you, Tom." Fred replied. "What do you think a wise leader should do in this situation?"

"Probably ask *WHY* they think the way that they do," answered Tom.

"Precisely," said Fred. "Because once you hear their rationale, you might not think that it's such a dumb idea anymore. But if it does, in fact, turn out to be a 'less than perfect' response, then 'asking why' will begin to highlight the flaws in their logic or rationale. You can then phrase your 'objections' in the form of other probing questions that might help your subordinates reformulate their opinion. Questions such as 'Have you thought about…' or 'what about….' Or 'did you consider…'. That way, if they really haven't thought about something, *a wise leader doesn't tell them what to do* or tell them the answer....rather, he or she just *helps them develop their thinking* while still acknowledging their contribution. After all, the last thing you want to have happen, Tom, is for your people to be afraid to give you their ideas. And they will if you make them feel bad for doing so...and especially for ideas and suggestions that YOU don't initially understand. So, when this happens just say: '*Thank you for telling me that* or for suggesting that. But I also need you to think a bit more on some of the problems that we discussed. Please get back to me when you have done so. But, thanks once again for the discussion. I enjoyed it.'

"I have to tell you, though, Tom," the wise old man continued, "I've sometimes been amazed at how deep a subordinate's thinking has gone regarding a particular problem that I've asked for an opinion on. My probing questions have actually caused me to reconsider the opinion that I originally started with. And guess what, I never had to reveal that it was me holding the 'dumb solution'. So, MY questions and THEIR great answers allowed me to test the logic behind my own solution. And, together, WE have developed many great solutions. So, then, we ALL get to 'feel good' about ourselves."

Fred suddenly reached into his desk drawer and handed Tom a sheet of paper. "Here, Tom" he said, "here's my list of questions that I've collected over the years that I think make a difference in how a leader operates. I use this list to remind myself about the important questions that I need to keep asking my people." It read:

IMPORTANT QUESTIONS WISE LEADERS ASK OFTEN:

What do you think/recommend?

Do you have any ideas or suggestions on ...?

How might we possibly....?

What's preventing us from...?

What's holding us back...?

Why do you think/feel this way?

Is there a better way?

What do you like most/least about us/our company/our
department/your job?

What would you change if you could?

Why are you/we doing this?

Why are you/we doing this, this way?

What do you want from this
organization/department/job?

What should we stop doing?

Fred looked at his watch. It was nearing noon and he had a lunch appointment to keep. He got up, put on his jacket and started walking towards the door. As he did so he said:

"You know, Tom, it's a funny business being a leader. You start out thinking that you are supposed to have all of the answers and you wind up realizing that you don't have that many...and too few good ones. But, a wise leader remembers the old adage that *'none of us is as smart as all of us'* and that his job is *to tap the creative and intellectual capital of all his people*. There's gold locked inside the heads of Rick and Harry. Go dig for it, Tom! They already know what they need to do. They already understand the mission's message. They just need your help in articulating and expressing those ideas."

'Thanks Fred," Tom said. "Any other advice".

"Sure...lots," the wise old man smiled. "But, for now, let me just add one thing. Whatever ideas or suggestions the three of you come up with - and eventually all agree upon - *you must make sure that they are very specific and measurable so that there is no confusion as to what anything means*. You want to be able to know whether their ideas are being implemented. You want to be able to *see* what they say they are going to do and to know whether it has been done - or not."

Tom followed Fred out to the elevator. The two men said good-bye to each other with Fred again offering to see Tom should he need to carry on the discussion.

Tom said, "No, Fred, I think I now know what I need to do and," he paused, "I guess so do Rick and Harry also...I just never realized it. Thanks Fred." With that, Tom turned away and took the stairs to the company's cafeteria to plan his afternoon with his two employees.

After lunch, Tom found Rick and Harry at their workstations and asked them if they wouldn't mind staying after work "for no more than thirty minutes" to discuss some issues that Tom was worried about. Both agreed. He also made a brief visit to the Customer Relations Department to organize a survey of expectations that customers might have when telephoning into the company. The meeting lasted over three hours. In the end, he was told that the survey and report containing the results would take about two months. "Fred was right again" thought Tom to himself and so he started to formulate his own action plan for understanding what customers want.

When it was 'quitting time', Tom brought both men into his office and said: "Thanks for agreeing to stay a few minutes extra, guys. I need your help."

"That's okay, Tom." interjected Harry. "We're happy to help you in any way that we can. What's up?"

Tom began, "I'm a bit concerned, Harry. You see, I believe that you both know the company's new mission."

"Absolutely", Rick exclaimed. "How could we not know it with everything that you've put us through to learn it? My wife said that I even mumbled it in my sleep last night".

They all laughed. Tom continued, "That's great, Rick! But, I've been thinking an awful lot about what we've been doing and I've come to the conclusion that it's just not enough to know and remember an important message like the mission. It's also important *to understand what the mission message means at a very personal level*. We have to know and understand *what the mission message means in terms of how we do our individual jobs*. Otherwise, it's just a bunch of words on a piece of paper and no one will really know what to do with it."

"I'm not sure that I buy what you're saying" said Rick, a bit disapprovingly.

"Why?" Tom replied.

"Because our mission says that we will 'provide products of the highest quality and service'. Our mission has nothing to do with me or Harry. It emphasizes the company's *products*. So the people most affected by the new mission are really the folks who make our products in the plants...and the technicians who service them...not a couple of telephone operators like us. Aren't I right, Harry?"

Harry was silent.

"I see", said Tom. "I now have a better picture of why you feel the way that you do and…by the way, thank you for telling me that. But, are you absolutely sure that the mission message, and I mean the whole mission message, has nothing to do with us?

Remember it says, 'Our mission is to provide products of the highest quality and service that will truly delight and amaze each and every customer that we are privileged to serve.' *Surely, there is some way that we can take those words, or even some of those words, and make them apply to us*. What do you think?"

After a few moments of silence, Harry piped up, "Well, I suppose the words 'delight and amaze each and every customer' could apply to my job."

"You know, Harry, I think you're right!" an excited Tom replied. And at that he took two pads of paper that were on his desk and handed one each to Rick and Harry. Tom then said, "Look guys. Please just humor and bear with me for a moment. But would you quickly jot down any ideas or suggestions that you have in terms of how you might, in your jobs as telephone operators, 'truly delight and amaze each and every one of our customers?'"

And remembering how Fred had done it with him, Tom added, "…and please don't pre-judge your answers. Just write down quickly whatever comes into your head." Tom decided to create a list for himself as well.

After a few minutes had passed, Tom asked Rick and Harry to each read their answers out loud while he recorded them on the flip chart beside his desk. He read his own list last. To everyone's amazement. Tom's list was the shortest and really didn't add anything extra. The summary of their responses looked as follows:

Rick's and Harry's Suggestions on how they might, as telephone operators, 'truly delight and amaze each and every one of our customers'

1. Answer the phone very quickly when it rings.
   ***

2. Answer with a very friendly and inviting greeting. ***

3. Answer with a very warm and friendly tone of voice. ***

4. Ask for the caller's name early and repeat it back many times. *

5. Never say "NO" to a caller.*

6. Sincerely apologize for having to put a caller "ON HOLD". **

7. Always thank the caller for calling. **

8. When ending a call - or transferring a call - do so with a sincere expression of appreciation. *

*'s = number of persons mentioning the item

All three men decided that they should combine items 7 & 8.

"What a fantastic list of ideas!" exclaimed Tom with a broad grin. "Which ones do you think that we should do?"

"All of them." proclaimed Harry enthusiastically.

"I agree", said Rick, a little more subdued, however.

"Do you really think that you can do all of them?" asked Tom.

"Absolutely!" Harry almost shouted.

Tom then thought of Fred's parting advice and said, "But, don't you think we also need to be a bit more specific for some of these?"

"What do you mean?" Harry responded.

"I mean that I think that **we should specify and agree on what it means to answer the phone quickly so that there is no confusion.** In other words, how many rings should the caller hear before we answer."

After a brief discussion, they all agreed that they should set the target number of rings - the standard - at two. They also agreed that they should try to say a caller's name a minimum of three times.

"And what about the greetings?" Tom added. "Do you think that *we should specify and agree on* the words in the initial telephone greeting as well as in the closing expression of appreciation?"

Both Rick and Harry seemed to chime "yes" together.

Tom then asked them to again use their pads and individually write out a proposed greeting and expression of appreciation that they might both eventually agree to use. Tom also wrote out a proposed greeting and 'expression' for himself. When they were finished, he wrote out the suggestions that each person had on the flip chart (*revealing his own versions last*) and together they 'massaged' the words into a final format.

The initial telephone greeting and expression of appreciation that they eventually agreed upon went as follows:

INITIAL TELEPHONE GREETING:

Good day and welcome to ABC Company. This is Rick/Harry. To whom do I have the pleasure of speaking?

Person responds with their name - or not.

If they do, we say:

Thank you for calling ABC Company, (add person's name- if available). How may I help you?

Then, say the person's name as frequently as possible (minimum three times).

****

EXPRESSION OF APOLOGY FOR PUTTING A CUSTOMER ON HOLD.

I am very sorry (Say name) and please excuse me, but I am going to have to put you 'on hold' for a moment. I promise to get back to you very quickly, thank you. And, once again, my apologies.

****

EXPRESSION OF APPRECIATION AT THE END OF EVERY CALL (or when transferring a call):

Thank you for calling ABC Company (say person's name) and it's been a pleasure talking with you today.

When they were done, Tom surveyed the list of suggestions that they had created and said, "Wow, I would think that any caller would be both delighted and amazed if you gave them everything on that list. Now, are you guys really sure that you can do all of them? Have we created something here that is realistic and doable?"

Both Rick and Harry expressed their agreement. They also vowed to each other that starting tomorrow, they would begin implementing all of the ideas that they had generated that afternoon. Harry even said that he would arrange to have formal printed copies of their ideas prepared and distributed. They then all gave each other 'high five' hand slaps and words of congratulation. Because it was getting late Tom told them to 'call it a day'. As Rick and Harry left his office, Tom beamed with delight. "Well," he thought, "they finally *know what to do*!"

The Second Question

The next several days proved to be extremely busy ones for Tom. It was the third quarter in his company's fiscal year and the company's annual planning cycle was in high gear. There were volumes of data that he needed to analyze and a half-dozen reports that he needed to generate. Tom wondered how he was going to get all of his "desk-work" done. So, he worked late into the evening most nights and came to work early every morning. Tom loved his new job and all of the new responsibilities that he was given. He would not allow himself to fail. Time sped by.

After a while, Tom thought that he should 'check-up' on Rick and Harry to see how they were doing. He disguised his voice and phoned into the company several times. He also stood nonchalantly outside the work stations where Rick and Harry resided to listen to them answering the phone.

Tom was dismayed with what he saw and heard. Only once was the phone answered on the second ring. Most of the time, it was four or five rings – and sometimes even longer. It was Tom's impression that these situations occurred because Rick and Harry would either be in the middle of a conversation that they did not wish to interrupt or that they were checking timesheets and did not want to pull themselves away from the task immediately at hand. He also witnessed several occasions in which courier drivers appeared to get more attention from the two telephone operators than their ringing phones.

As for the other mission task items, Tom observed that while Harry appeared to be trying to use the various telephone greetings and expressions, Rick, on the other hand, never did. Both Rick and Harry also seemed to say "NO" a lot to their callers. And, as for both men's tone of voice, it was, in Tom's opinion neither warm nor friendly. "They sound like barking dogs" thought Tom. "So, why aren't they doing what the company needs them to do?....what they agreed to do?"

Tom then remembered Fred's famous first question to him: **"Do they know what to do?"** So he decided to test this for himself. He asked both Rick and Harry if they knew the mission. They claimed that they did and when he asked them to recite it, they did so flawlessly. Tom then asked them if they knew what the mission meant in terms of their jobs. It was here that Tom discovered a problem. Neither Rick nor Harry could recite the list of tasks - the mission task list, as he called it - that they had generated and agreed to follow when answering the telephone. "Holy cow," thought Tom, "they still don't *know what to do*. This is a lot tougher than I thought."

Tom, however, was better prepared this time. He told Rick and Harry that he was disappointed in their knowledge of the mission task list; that he was going to treat it in the same way that he had dealt with the mission; and, that he expected them both to memorize it and to be able to recite it. "After all," said the clever young man to both of them, "if you can't say it, you can't live it." Both Rick and Harry agreed with this and promised to memorize the "MTL" (Harry's new name for the mission task list).

Over the next week, Tom took Rick and Harry each morning through a sort of 'morning roll call' on the mission and MTL. The first few days met with some mild resistance. But Tom was determined and he told both Rick and Harry that he was going to *relentlessly make them repeat the list over and over again* until they succeeded. And in a short while they did. "We were cajoled into submission", Harry told his lunchmates in the cafeteria one day.

"Ahhh," thought Tom rather confidently, "now they really *know what to do*." But, he was soon to be disappointed again. His subsequent informal checks on how well Rick and Harry were performing the mission task list showed that nothing had really changed. "They *know what to do*", Tom said to himself "however, they are still not doing what the company needs them to do…what they agreed to do." Tom was dejected.

As luck would have it, though, Tom found himself in a meeting the next day in which the wise old man was present. As they broke for lunch, Fred asked Tom, "So, my clever young man, how are things going with Rick and Harry?"

"I'm afraid that they're still not doing what the company need them to do." he said.

"But, *do they know what to do*?" asked the wise old man.

"Yes," said Tom, "they absolutely *know what to do*. There is no doubt in my mind." And he then recounted for Fred all of his efforts to translate the mission message. He recounted the mission task list that Rick and Harry had both generated, agreed to and memorized.

"Okay, it sounds like they both know what to do. But, *do they know why they should be doing these things*?" retorted the wise old man.

"Do they know why they should be doing these things?" repeated Tom with an incredulous tone in his voice. "I should certainly hope so."

"Well, you better make sure." Fred replied, "because, **when people understand 'the why' about something that they have to do, they tend to work at it more than when they don't.** If Rick and Harry don't understand 'the why', it will be a lot harder for them to accept the new tasks. So, if I were you, I would make sure that they both **know why they need to do what they agreed to do.**"

The meeting then resumed leaving Tom to reflect on the wise old man's latest question.

Since Tom was swamped with his own work, he decided to wait a few days before he spoke with Rick and Harry. He would use the time to collect his thoughts on what he wanted to say to them. But, he also wanted to conduct his own informal survey of telephone callers, telling them about the company mission and asking them for ideas on how the company might live up to its promise to 'delight and amaze' them when phoning in. If no suggestions were immediately forthcoming, Tom would prompt them by going over the mission task list and asking their opinion about each item. To his utter surprise, there were no new items introduced. Interestingly, most thought that the idea of 'never saying no' was silly and impracticable.

About ten days later, Tom asked his two subordinates to come in a bit early so that they could "talk about some things". He even arranged to have a light breakfast ready for them when they arrived. But, Tom also remembered some of the wise old man's earlier advice about what everyone wants: *to feel good about themselves, to feel that what they do matters and to feel 'respected, and appreciated'*, just like the mission statement says. And so he began, "First of all let me say that I have really appreciated all the support that you have given me in some of the initiatives that I have tried to institute since getting my new job. I know that sometimes, it's probably not been easy working with me. You're the first people that I have ever had to manage and so I know that I'm probably making a lot of mistakes. However, I want to thank you for your patience with me. I have to tell you, though, I'm having to learn a lot of stuff really quickly and I hope you know how much I will continue to need your help and advice as we go along."

"We do, Tom" said Harry "and, thank you for telling us this."

"I also have some interesting information to share with you" continued Tom and he then proceeded to tell them about the results of his informal survey of customer needs. "So you see guys" he said, "I think my survey shows that we were able to second guess our customers' needs fairly well...and, so congratulations...However, given the response I got concerning the 'never say no' idea from the mission task list, what do you think we should do?"

After some humorous conversation around this particular item, Rick recommended that they drop the item from the MTL. Harry echoed his support for Rick's recommendation with the words, "I second the motion!"

"Okay," said Tom, "I concur...But, I also have a problem." Tom paused for effect. "I know that both you guys know what the company needs you to do in your job as telephone operators. You both know the mission......right?"

"We sure do." replied Rick.

"And you both now can recite the mission task list that you both agreed you'd do....don't you?

"Right, again" answered Harry.

"Then, for pete's sake, why the heck aren't you guys doing them?" a frustrated Tom asked. He then told them how his informal checks revealed that there were problems in implementing all of the new changes that they had agreed to.

Turning specifically to Rick, Tom said, "And you, Rick...you seem to be having more problems than Harry....why? Why are you not doing what you agreed to do? Please tell me so that I can at least understand."

"Well, if you must know," Rick stammered, "I find that I feel kind of silly doing these things. I know that you spent some time explaining how we could make a connection or link between our jobs as telephone operators and the new mission. But, I still don't see why we have to do this. All mission statements are just a load of B.S. anyway and it seems to me that you're just forcing us to do something that really doesn't matter……that won't make a difference one way or the other. And, as I said before, I really think the new mission, if it means anything, is intended more for the guys in the plants and the service techies. Not a pair of telephone operators, like us. Right, Harry?"

"I hate to admit it, Tom," Harry replied, "but I kind of agree with Rick. I really don't feel comfortable doing many of the things on our mission task list and they seem a bit forced, if you know what I mean. So, like Rick, *I just don't see the need for doing them.*"

Tom was completely taken aback and thought, "The wise old man was right, they don't know why they should be doing what the company needs them to do." He then said: "Well, this has come as quite a surprise to me guys. But, thank you for your honesty and trust. Thank you for telling me how you both feel. Now let me ask you something." Tom paused: "Can you please tell me why any company exists?"

"Sure…that's easy," laughed Rick. "To make money."

"And you're absolutely right" replied Tom. "If a company does not make any money it will not exist. It will not survive. It will not have the money either to re-invest into itself or to pay the stockholders a return on their investment. But paying dividends is something that a company does at the 'end of the process', don't you agree? What I want you to tell me is what every company has to do *to come into existence*. What is it that every company must do, at the beginning, in order to exist...and if it fails to do that, it will not exist?"

"That's easy too," answered Harry. "A company exists because it's able to satisfy a need."

"Right again" Tom proclaimed excitedly. "A company comes into existence because it is able to satisfy the needs of a customer. If a company is not able to satisfy - and *continue* to satisfy - a customer's needs, it will not attract new customers - or retain old ones. It will then not make money and it will not exist. So, satisfying customer needs is pretty important, wouldn't you say?"

Both Rick and Harry murmured their agreement.

"And that's where our new mission statement comes in." Tom continued. "We have that mission because the company wanted to communicate to every employee what it is that we currently **need to *focus on*** in order to exist....in other words, to attract, win and retain customers. The mission begins the process of telling us what we need to do. It also captures the spirit and attitude we need to have in order to do that."

"Okay," said Rick, "but, like I said before, what's that got to do with me...or Harry?"

"Everything!" shouted Tom. "Don't you see, Rick, we're not the only game in town, right? We live in a competitive world. Our customers have choices and that means we have competition. It's kind of like living in the 'singles scene'...we never really marry any of our customers, we just date them...and we want our customers to keep dating us. So, now I have to ask you how you think our customers - let alone any customer - goes about deciding which company to do business with...which company to date?"

Harry chuckled at the analogy and said, "Probably, the one who always makes sure that they have a good time...and the one that satisfies their overall needs the best."

"Absolutely!" Tom responded. "And that's why our mission statement doesn't just simply say that we want to satisfy our customers, but rather that we want to 'truly delight and amaze' them. Now, how do you think we might go about proving to a customer that we are serious about what we are saying...that we are telling the truth in our mission and not just promoting some clever sounding phrases or slogans?"

"That's not too hard a question either," Harry answered. "A customer can tell by the way the company treats them...by the way that the company acts and responds to their needs."

"I agree with you 100 per cent", Tom replied enthusiastically. "*Actions speak louder than words.* It's a notion that has been around for a very long time. In fact, you can even find many references to it in the Bible. One of my favorites is from James 2:13-20 in which he asks 'what is faith'. I think the best line James has is when he states, '*Show me thy faith without thy works and I will show you my faith by my works...because, faith without works is dead.*'"

"Amen" Harry rejoined emphatically. Tom smiled. Rick, on the other hand, appeared glum.

Turning to him directly, Tom said: "Rick, our mission statement is our *statement of faith*. But for the mission statement to come alive, to be more than just a set of nice sounding words, *we have to live the mission and to make it part of our everyday activities.* That's why we had to translate the mission so that it could be understood...and practiced. But, surely, if we are going to 'truly delight and amaze each and every customer', as our mission says, it's going to require the effort and actions of more than just one or two people. And it's going to require the effort and actions of more than just the people in the plants. It's going to take all of us. ***It's not just enough for one or two people in our company to live the mission. We all have to.*** And that's why it's important, even for a couple of telephone operators, to do their part in helping to make the mission come alive. Do you see what I'm saying?"

"I think I'm beginning to see what you mean." said Rick softly.

"Let me now show you something else to help reinforce my point" continued Tom and he got up and walked over to his flip chart. He then drew the following sketch on the top page and said: "Rick, I want you to imagine that this is a picture of a beach somewhere, with a bunch of seagulls resting quietly on the shore.

"Now imagine what would happen if a big dog were suddenly to emerge and, seeing the seagulls, it decided to charge the resting flock. What do you think would happen? Describe the picture that you would see." Tom asked.

"There'd be chaos" said Rick.

"Definitely!" smiled Tom and he then proceeded to complete his picture with wild-like strokes.

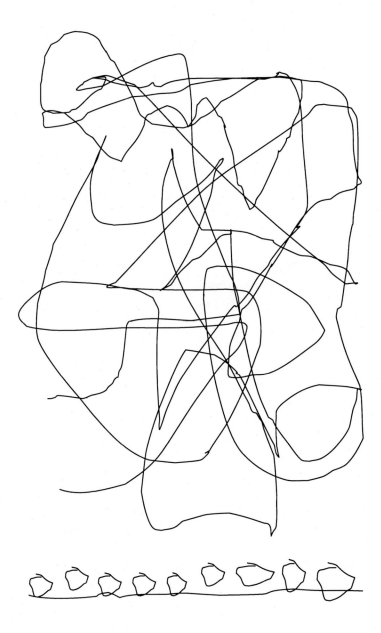

Tom flipped the page over and drew the first picture again. He then said: "Okay, now I want you to imagine the same beach...only this time it has a different set of birds on it...they're called Canadian Geese. Have you ever seen one?"

"Yeah," Harry blurted out. "They're pretty big birds with...kind of fat bodies. Grey in color, I think."

"That's pretty close," said Tom. "As a matter of fact, the birds are really heavy. But the remarkable thing about them is that each year, they make a journey with a round-trip distance of around 8000 miles. In the fall, they travel from their home in Canada to spend the winter in Mexico...and then return in the spring. It's an incredible journey. Now, many people have speculated as to what could possibly enable such birds - birds that look 'aerodynamically challenged' - to accomplish such a feat. It is generally believed that it has a lot to do with how they fly together."

Tom poised his flip chart pen at the ready and said: "So imagine that we are on that same beach, but with the Canadian Geese there this time, and the same dog comes along and charges them. Could either one of you describe for me what the picture would look like after a few minutes?"

Both Rick and Harry remained silent.

Tom responded for them. "The birds would quickly adopt a flying formation that would look something like this." He then proceeded to make the following sketch...

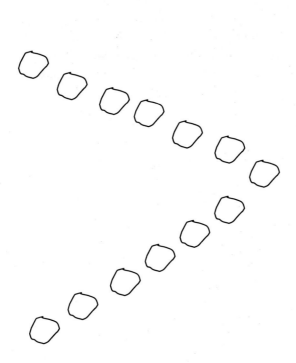

"They would create this 'V' formation," Tom continued, "which, incidentally, is how you can always recognize Canadian Geese when you see them in flight...especially during the migration season. However, it is also believed that by flying in this 'V' formation, it is one of the most important things that make it possible for the birds to complete their annual journey so efficiently. You see, the lead bird has primary responsibility for setting the direction for the flock and for navigation. The only problem is that it takes the full brunt of the wind's force and tires very quickly. When this happens a special maneuver takes place in which the lead bird rotates to the back of the flock's 'V' formation and the next bird in line takes over 'flying point'.

"Now, what's so special about rotating to the back position, you ask? The theory goes that as each bird flaps its huge wings, it creates a minor up-draft, or up-lift, for the birds following behind...and that the effect is cumulative. In other words, the strongest uplift from all the birds flapping their wings is felt at the very back - which just happens to be the place where the bird that is most tired goes to recuperate after flying point.

"It is believed that the net result of this particular flying formation and rotation maneuver is that the entire flock is able to cover a significantly greater flying distance each day more efficiently than if each bird was trying to make the journey on its own.

"But the key to the birds' success lies in the fact that each bird instinctively knows what it must do to help the whole flock accomplish its mission. Each bird knows and understands the importance of *staying in formation* and each bird *knows the important role that it plays - whatever its position - in terms of helping the entire flock achieve its goals both more effectively and efficiently.*"

"See this bird, here", Tom said as he pointed emphatically to one of the middle circles that he had drawn in the 'V' formation. "This bird does not say to itself 'What I do doesn't matter.' It doesn't say, 'No one really cares whether I stay in formation or not.' Instead, it knows that what it does, no matter how small it may seem to be, contributes to the success of the flock and that if it were to break formation, it could jeopardize the entire 'organization'.

"And so, I guess what I am trying to emphasize here for you Rick - and for you too Harry - is that what you do in your jobs at this company matters an awful lot in terms of achieving our mission. You both have a vital and important role to play in your jobs as telephone operators in helping to make the mission come alive and in satisfying our customers. After all, you're the first persons that customers have contact with when they phone our company. You're their first experience with our company's mission. If customers get 'turned-off' based on how we treat them when they phone us, they may decide that they don't want to do business with us. And so, we all have a part to play, guys, when it comes to making the mission real. If we are really going to become a company that 'truly delights and amazes' our customers then its going to require a contribution from each and every one of us. Not just from some of us, but from all of us…and all of the time. Do you get it?'

"I never really thought about it that way," said Rick.

"That's okay," said Tom. "I'm just sorry that we didn't have this conversation earlier. It might have made things a lot easier in terms of *knowing why* I was doing some of the things that I did…and *knowing why* I needed you to do certain things in a certain way. I'm sorry for not explaining '*the why*' better."

"But now also know this," Tom continued. "I really do value what you and Harry are doing and I continue to need your help if we are going to become a mission-driven organization - one that truly delights and amazes each and every customer. Can I count on you?"

"You can count on us, right Rick?" said Harry.

"You betcha!" Rick responded.

"Yikes! Look at the time!" exclaimed Harry. "We've got about sixty seconds to open the company switchboard. We better get going, Tom, or we will wind up amazing our customers the wrong way for sure."

Tom laughed. "Okay", he said "and, once again guys, thanks for coming in early." Rick and Harry then scurried out of Tom's office and dashed down the corridor.

Tom was pleased. *"They know what to do."* he thought, rather contentedly. *"And they now know why they should do it. Now, they will do what the company needs them to do…*what they agreed to do".

Later in the morning, Harry came to Tom's office during his break and dropped off some summary notes that he thought would help him remember some of the ideas that Tom had passed on to him. Tom's spirits soared as he reviewed Harry's handiwork. It read:

Making our Mission come alive

The primary mission of every company is to satisfy the needs of customers.

The company that satisfies customers the best, wins.

Talk is cheap. We must show our customers that we love them.
Actions speak louder than words.

Satisfying customers is the responsibility of every person.

I can make a difference by how I act.
I can make a contribution to the success of the mission in my job.

STAY IN FORMATION!

The Third Question

As the days passed, Tom tried to find as many opportunities as possible to see how Rick and Harry were doing. He continued to ask them to recite the mission and their mission task list every few days, which both men continued to excel at. He was also very pleased to find that both Rick and Harry seemed to say the new greeting and expression of appreciation during each call without exception and with ease. It was his perception, however, that problems continued to exist in terms of answering the phone within two rings and always repeating the customer's name. He also thought that Harry seemed to be putting more effort into these tasks than Rick.

The problem area that concerned Tom the most, though, was the tone of voice that each man used in speaking to the callers. Tom thought that their voices "sounded a bit grating", as he put it and "not nearly warm and friendly *enough*". "I wonder if they still don't **know what to do** on this one," he thought to himself. Tom, therefore, decided to speak to both men about this issue one morning in his office before they opened the switchboard...

****

"What do you mean, 'I have a problem with the way that you're speaking to the customers?'" asked Rick, a bit annoyed. "What's wrong now? Aren't we saying the right words that you wanted us to?"

Tom could sense that he had entered into a touchy area. "Yes", he replied, "you're saying the right words alright, but not the way that the company needs you to say them. It's really more about the tone of voice that you use."

"Our tone of voice?" Harry asked with a perplexed expression on his face "what's wrong with our tone of voice?"

"Well" Tom replied "It's my impression that you guys are not being very warm and friendly with the tone of voice that you are using when speaking to callers. Oh sure, you say all the right words that we agreed to…but, it seems to me that the tone you're using is much too flat. It just doesn't seem friendly and inviting enough."

"What the heck does that mean?" said Rick clearly growing impatient.

"I thought you might say that," Tom rejoined. "So, I did some research and found three telephone numbers of companies who, in my opinion, answer the phone with operators who use a very warm and friendly tone. But first let me play for you how the two of you sound to a caller."

Tom then turned to the new telephone on his desk which had the extra feature of a mini tape-recorder built in. It was connected to the company's main telephone lines so that Tom could now listen in on the conversations that the two telephone operators were having with callers. He pressed the play button. It was Rick's voice that they heard first giving the agreed-upon greeting. It blared out over the speakerphone. Then it was Harry's turn. Both men agreed that that was how they typically sounded when they answered the phone.

Tom then dialed the first of the telephone numbers that he wanted to use as role models. The difference from how Rick and Harry answered the phone was startling. While the words used to greet callers were not as compelling as the ones that they had crafted, the telephone operator's voice itself was, as Harry put it, 'silky smooth'.

The next two examples were equally instructive. And in between each call, Tom played the recording that he had made of Rick and Harry to further highlight and reinforce the differences with the way that they spoke.

"Now do you *see* what I mean?" asked Tom.

Rick grew flushed and seemed ready to explode. "Listen here, Tom" he said with a strained voice. "This is the only voice that I got and I've used it my whole life. It hasn't caused me any trouble up until now and, quite frankly, sir, you seem to be the only person that has a problem with it."

Tom remained calm and responded quietly. "Please, Rick, I am not trying to upset you." He paused. "…and please forgive me if I am doing so. It's just that you both agreed a while back…when we put the mission task list together, remember?…that we should always try to answer the phone with a warm and friendly tone of voice…isn't that what we agreed?"

Both Rick and Harry remained silent.

"And why are we doing this?"

"To delight and amaze our customers," said Harry, jumping in.

"That's right" Tom smiled. "So, the only thing that I am doing here, right now, is trying to give you guys some feedback on this one area and to give you a better idea of what you need to do in order to answer the phone with a warm and friendly tone of voice. You're both doing a great job with the greetings and I really appreciate that you are saying them so diligently. I just think that you need to work a little harder and concentrate more on how you say those words…Okay? As a matter of fact, let me give you my own version of what I think it means to answer the phone with a warm and friendly voice."

And at that, Tom picked up his telephone and pretended that there was a caller phoning in.

"Good afternooooon and welcome to ABC Company" he purred. "This is Tom," he said, almost breathlessly. "To whom do I have the pleasure of speaking?" Tom's voice was now an incredible, yet pleasant mixture of modulating and soft tones. It was definitely, though, not Tom's usual speaking voice. He then went on to repeat the simulated caller's name many times. He pretended to put the caller on hold and then signed-off with the agreed upon expression.

When he was finished with his mock call, Tom looked at Rick and Harry and said, "There...now do you have a clearer picture of what I am talking about? Do you *see* what I am saying?"

"And you expect us to do that?" asked Rick with a hint of incredulity in his voice.

"Absolutely," Tom replied "and do you know why?"

"I suppose so," said Rick.

"No, Rick," came Tom's swift rejoinder. "Don't suppose. Know! Tell me why we need to do things the way that we said…the way that we specified in the mission task list. Prove to me that you know why we are doing what we are doing."

Rick stumbled though his response. But, he still managed to cover the main points of Tom's earlier speech about satisfying the customer and satisfying the customer better than the competition.

Tom was pleased. "At least he knows 'the why'," he thought to himself. "Look guys," he continued aloud, "I've tried to show you how other companies are doing it. I've even shown you that I can do it, if I need to…And if I can do this, so can you. So please, give it another try. Try to be more friendly and more warm. I know that you both can do this if you want to…alright?"

"Okay," said Harry.

"Sure, Tom," responded Rick. But it was Tom's impression as Rick left the office that his response sounded less than whole-hearted.

Over the next few days, Tom tried to observe if there were any noticeable changes in the way that Rick and Harry spoke to their callers. Harry took up the challenge right away. But Tom became concerned when it appeared that Harry was experimenting with a variety of different voices. Harry also seemed to be losing the confidence that Tom thought he used to sense in him when Harry answered the phone. Rick, on the other hand, seemed to try at first, but then quickly gave up. Tom grew despondent as he realized that he had reached yet another stumbling block with his two charges.

What to do? As he had not spoken with his old mentor in a while, Tom decided once again to give Fred a call and see what advice the wise old man might have for him. Fred, as usual, stated that he was glad to hear from the clever young man that he so much admired and suggested that they meet for lunch the next day.

As they sat down at their table in the company cafeteria, Fred asked, "So, Tom, how goes the battle?"

"Not very well," he replied. "I'm still having problems with Rick and Harry".

"*Do they know what to do*?" said the wise old man.

"Undeniably," Tom responded. "They know the mission. They understand the mission. And they know what they specifically have to do to make a contribution to the mission in their jobs. I know this for sure."

"And *do they know why they need to do it?*" pressed the wise old man.

"Unquestionably," said Tom. "I have spent a lot of time explaining *'the why'* to them and I know that they both understand the role that they have to play in making the mission a reality." Tom then recounted for the wise old man all of the stories and anecdotes that he had shared with his two employees. He concluded by saying: "but they're still not doing everything that the company needs them to do." Tom then relayed his frustration over his inability to have Rick and Harry answer the phone with a warm and friendly tone of voice.

"I see," said the wise old man. "But do they know how to do what you are asking them to do? *Do they know how to do it?*"

"How to do it?" Tom repeated back. "Absolutely!" He then described how he had shown Rick and Harry the three role model examples of telephone operators at other companies. He also told

Fred about his own personal demonstration of answering the phone.

When Tom was finished, the wise old man said, "That's very impressive, Tom. But, it seems to me that all you have really done is shown them more "what to do" stuff and then proved to them that you can do it. Rick and Harry, however, may still not know how to do what it is that you are asking them to do. It's kind of like swimming, Tom. You can have lots of people demonstrate their forward crawl for you and still not really know how to do it …As a matter of fact, I'm not sure if I could do what you are asking Rick or Harry to do…or, do it the right way, at least…and the reason is because I really don't know how to do what you are asking me to do."

"I think I'm beginning to see what you mean", said Tom.

"Now," Fred continued, "if I asked you – or told you - to do something that you felt you didn't know how to do, what do you think the natural reaction of most people would be?"

"Fear."

"And what do you think that they might be afraid of Tom?"

"They could be afraid of a lot of things," Tom answered nervously. "Afraid of failing. Afraid of looking stupid or dumb."

"And why are most people afraid of looking stupid, Tom?" pressed the wise old man.

"Because," said Tom remembering a previous lesson from Fred, "they then won't *feel good about themselves.* They'll feel inadequate."

"So what then do they do, Tom? What action are they most likely to take?"

"Why...they do nothing. They just keep on doing what they have done before."

"Exactly!" said Fred pointedly. "Most people are afraid of the things that they haven't done before because it means that they have to leave what I like to call their *'comfort zone of the familiar'*...the stuff that they already know how to do...the stuff that already makes them feel good about themselves. Sometimes, when you ask them to do something that they don't know how to do, they might even think that you are setting them up for failure...as a reason to get rid of them... Or maybe they even tried it once before and they failed and now they are convinced that it can't be done...that they cannot do it... And so *you have to help them get past their fears.* Remember what I told you earlier, Tom. *A leader helps his subordinates*…and one of the most important things that a leader can do is *to help drive out the fear that they have when you ask them to do something new or unfamiliar.* You need to help Rick and Harry by making certain that they *know how to do what you need them to do.* Only then can you really be sure that the reason they are not doing what you want them to do is not because they are afraid of failing….or because they have convinced themselves that they will fail!"

"But how could they have convinced themselves that they would fail?"

"Let me answer that with an analogy, Tom... Have you ever wondered why huge circus elephants will stand still while tethered to just a small stake in the ground? As far as you or I are concerned, we know for sure that if the elephant wanted to wander about, that small stake would not be strong enough to hold it in place. So why then doesn't the elephant simply lift its huge foot and go wherever it wants? The answer it seems is that the elephant is somehow convinced that it cannot escape…that the stake is stronger than he is. And, 'why does the elephant think this way?' you ask. Because when the elephant was a baby, that stake was indeed strong enough. And every time the elephant tried to get away, it found that it could not succeed. So, after many attempts and an equal number of failures, the elephant became convinced that it could not overcome the strength of the stake. Then the elephant grows up. But because of all its past experiences, it never tries to escape because it is convinced that it can't....so, the elephant doesn't even try....Too often, Tom, people will also act like those circus elephants. Because of 'bad' past experiences, they think 'bad' thoughts about themselves...there's this little voice inside their heads telling them that they're no good, that they're failures and that they shouldn't even try because they'll fail just like all the other times they tried. Good leaders, however, help to silence that voice and in so doing help their followers to see new possibilities...the new possibilities of success! In order for that to happen, a good leader makes sure his followers *know how to do what they are being asked to do.* Have I answered your question, Tom?"

"Totally, and once again Fred, you've given me some outstanding advice....Thank you," Tom said admiringly.

"That's okay Tom," Fred warmly responded. "But, remember what Mark Twain once said about advice."

"What's that?"

"That it's better to give than to receive."

The two men laughed at Fred's remark and carried on with their lunch...

When Tom later returned to his work area, he asked both Rick and Harry to stay, once again, for a few minutes after work. They both agreed. Tom decided to use part of his afternoon getting ready for his meeting with them. When the appointed time arrived, Rick and Harry strolled into Tom's office together.

"What's up, boss?" Harry chirped and slumped down into one of the chairs beside Tom's desk. Rick decided to remain standing.

"Guys," Tom began "I'm sorry that I had to ask you to stay late yet again. But, I'm still having a problem with the way that you're both answering the phone...in particular, with the tone of voice that you're both using."

"Oh, no!" cried Rick "Not this again. What's wrong with my tone now? You know that I've been trying."

"Yeah," Harry joined in, "Me too! As a matter of fact, I'm starting to drive myself crazy with it. Rick says that I am starting to sound like a person with a split personality...Several of them."

The three of them laughed.

"Relax guys," Tom said. "I'm here to tell you that I know you've been trying. But I also want to ask you one thing."

"What's that?" the two men seemed to blurt out simultaneously.

"I want to know if you **know how to do** what I am asking you to do?"

"Not really," said Harry, who then added, "or, at least, I'm not sure if I'm doing it the right way."

"What about you, Rick?" Tom asked.

"Well," came his reply, "I know what you want me to do and why you want me to do it but I'm not sure that I can do it. I don't feel really confident."

"I thought so," said Tom. "So I want to take your worries away…for the both of you." And at that Tom proceeded to tell them that he had arranged for a speech therapist to come in for an hour every other afternoon. The therapist would work with them individually for about two weeks and help them to "smooth out the warbles in their voices".

Both Rick and Harry agreed that such training sessions would probably help a lot in terms of showing them how to regulate the tones in their voices, standardizing how they would both speak and giving them more confidence for doing this new task. They ended by thanking Tom "for not giving up on them". And with that, Tom told the two men to hurry home to their families and to keep him informed on how they liked the training.

Tom left his office very happy that evening.

The Fourth Question

The next day, as Tom had promised, the speech therapist arrived. At first, he just observed Rick and Harry. Later, he took each man aside into a vacant office and did some facial and neck exercises with them. He taught them how to hold their heads and how to tense certain muscles in their necks and throats. For the next session, he brought in an oscilloscope and used the machine to further instruct the two telephone operators. These sessions continued on for the next two weeks. The results, however, were immediately noticeable...and dramatic. Both Rick and Harry had altered the tone in their voices. As Tom listened to them answer calls, he felt that the money spent on the therapist was well worth the final product. The therapist had done his job.

"Rick and Harry certainly know how to answer the phone with a warm and friendly tone", Tom said to himself.

And so it came as somewhat of a surprise, when Tom listened in on their calls a week later, to find that Rick had basically abandoned his recent voice training and returned to his old way of answering the phone. Harry, on the other hand, appeared to have remained true to the lessons that he had learned. In fact, he seemed to revel in the new voice that he had discovered inside himself. Harry called it his "stage voice" and he would often amuse his colleagues in the cafeteria switching back and forth between the two voices. In fact, rumor had it that Harry was occasionally getting requests from some of his callers to meet him.

Tom, however, considered Harry's changes only to be a partial victory. He was still disturbed by the fact that both men continued to have problems with answering the phone quickly and continuously repeating a caller's name. In mulling the situation over in his mind, Tom reached the conclusion that both Rick and Harry "certainly had to know how to do these tasks" but that, for some reason, they were not doing them as they had previously agreed.

He decided to speak to Fred yet once again…..

****

"Do they *know what to do*?" the wise old man patiently asked.

"Yes," Tom replied.

"And, do they *know why they should do it*?"

"Definitely," answered Tom.

"And do they *know how to do it*?"

"Unquestionably" came the response.

"I see," said the wise old man. "But, do they *know that they should care about doing it*?"

"Do they know that they should care?" said an exasperated Tom. "They darn well should care! Look at everything that I have done with them…the constant drilling, the explaining, the repetition, and the training…. What more could I do?"

"Well," said the wise old man, "for starters you can make sure that both Rick and Harry know that they are being measured regularly in terms of the tasks that you want them to perform. They should know how well they are performing and they should know that you know too. Otherwise, they might simply think that nobody's watching them and, therefore, that nobody else cares, so why should they? Even worse, they might actually think that they're doing a good job…after all, who's to disprove them? And so they don't think that there's a need to change their behavior."

"But, but…" sputtered Tom, "I already do that. I listen in on their phone calls regularly. From time to time I also stand by their work area to try and overhear them speaking to callers. I sometimes even disguise my voice and make 'fake-calls' into the company. I then tell them what I have found out."

"That's fine, Tom," said the wise old man, "but it sounds to me that you're simply acting like a cop hiding in the bushes waiting to hand out speeding tickets. Let me ask you this," he paused. "Apart from you, how do Rick and Harry know how good a job they are doing? How do they know when they are doing a good job - so that they can keep on doing it - and when they are not - so that they can take corrective action on their own?"

"I'm not sure," said the clever young man. "I suppose that I just rely on them to monitor their own actions when I am not around."

"And you should. But, exactly how are they supposed to do that especially when they are in the thick of things?" came Fred's swift rejoinder. "Imagine a competitive sport Tom in which no one on the team - and no one in the audience - knows the score of a game until the very end…or until a referee simply decides to tell everyone. It would be very hard to play, not much fun to watch and make it difficult deciding when to cheer or change strategy. So you need some kind of mechanism that let's the players - and the referees - know the score as the game proceeds. ...

"Now, the same holds true for Rick and Harry. They need to *know on a regular and consistent basis how they are both performing and progressing…and especially whether they are getting better or worse over time* at what they are doing… and not just at a particular moment. That way, they can better react to whatever feedback they get in a more timely fashion and not just when it's too late to do anything about it….when the game is almost over."

"I see. And so, if I do what you've just told me," Tom interjected "will Rick and Harry start to *care* about what they are doing and what the company needs them to do?"

"Not always," answered the wise old man.

"What do you mean?"

"I mean that sometimes the feedback you give your subordinates isn't always enough to *motivate them to really care*…to do what you and the company need them to do. And that's because there's still another reason why they might not care."

"And what's that?"

"It has to do with *consequences*, Tom. For some people, if there are no *personal consequences associated with doing, or not doing, certain assigned tasks and behaviors,* they will not be as committed to doing them as they might otherwise be. So, when this happens to any of your subordinates, you have to figure out a way to let them know that what they choose to do - or not - really matters...and that it *matters to them personally...not just to the company.*"

"What kind of consequences?" asked Tom. "Do you mean money?"

"Yes and no," answered the wise old man with a sly grin growing on his face. "There's no doubt that money can be a powerful reward mechanism ...and have a very strong effect when it is withheld. But, there are also other ways to really motivate people. And, the one that I have found to be the most useful for creating positive consequences is *personal recognition,* - you know, the private and public praisings and tributes, as well as the pins, plaques, trophies, certificates and medals which show someone how much he or she is valued, appreciated and loved by the organization."

"Oh, like the pictures on the wall of some companies honoring their employee of the month," Tom enquired.

"That's right. But I have to warn you Tom that it's also important for any personal recognition to be *sincerely given.* You mustn't create a situation in which it's simply somebody's turn to get his or her picture on the wall. Otherwise it will not have its intended effect."

"I see."

Fred continued. "Tom, it's been my experience that we all really crave personal recognition and that when we don't get the recognition and respect that we feel we deserve, we generally use money to try and compensate for it....which is quite ironic, don't you think?"

"In what way?" Tom replied.

"It's ironic because there is usually only so much money that an organization has at its disposal to dole out for salary increases and merit bonuses....whereas personal recognition - in all its forms - costs practically nothing to give, is in almost unlimited supply and yet, seems to be the one thing that most managers and supervisors are very reluctant to hand out to their subordinates... which is unfortunate, because there is almost an infinite variety of ways…more than you or I could ever think up… in which you could give someone the personal recognition and respect that they desire…as long as they've earned it."

"This is really good advice, as usual," remarked Tom. "But, why didn't you tell me about this 'caring stuff' when I first came to see you to discuss my problems with Rick and Harry."

"Because," answered the wise old man "the leadership problems that you described earlier with Rick and Harry often simply disappear once people *'know what to do', ' know why they should do it' and 'know how to do it'*. Remember what I once told you about what everyone wants from his or her job?

"To feel good about themselves and to feel that what they do matters."

"Exactly," said Fred. "Well, when people know *'the what'* and *'the how"* of their job, they will usually do what you ask them to do because you've helped them feel both competent and confident in doing it. In other words, they feel good about themselves. And once they know *'the why'*, they can also feel good about themselves because they know that what they are doing counts….that it makes a difference… and they can see the role that they have to play in helping the whole organization succeed. Sometimes, once all these pieces are in place, they will find or invent their own rewards for doing what you need them to do."

"Come to think of it," Tom interrupted, "Harry does seem to enjoy entertaining people with his ability to switch his voice back and forth. He's found his own positive consequence from the voice change... once he knew how to do it."

"Absolutely!" bellowed the wise old man. "However, when you find yourself at a point where 'the what', 'the why' and 'the how' are all in place and you're still not getting the behaviors and actions that you as their leader want and need, you shouldn't despair because your efforts haven't been wasted. That's because you need to *have 'the what', 'the why' and 'the how' in place first before you can start setting up mechanisms to help them realize that they should care*. Otherwise, you are just setting them up to fail."

"To fail?" Tom asked.

"Yes, to fail, Tom," Fred paused. "Think about it. How would you like to have a job in which your boss told you there'd be a reward for doing something, but you didn't understand exactly what it was that he wanted you to do... and he wouldn't tell you either. Or, how would you like to work for someone who told you there'd be a consequence for not doing something properly, but you didn't know how to do it and no one would show you? *A leader has to make sure that his subordinates know 'the what', 'the why' and 'the how' first.* Only when these are in place can he start setting-up the *measurement systems and consequences* that make them know that they should care."

At that moment, Fred's secretary, Betty, knocked gently on the door and informed him that his four o'clock appointment with Ms. Reeves was at hand. Fred looked at Tom and apologized for having to cut their dialogue short. He then quickly left the room through a side door leaving Tom in his chair to contemplate everything that Fred had just told him.

Several days passed as Tom thought through his plans to help Rick and Harry *care about what they were doing*. His thinking, however, was interrupted by some encouraging news. The latest customer satisfaction survey results showed that, for the first time, customers were no longer generally "dissatisfied" with their telephone experience when calling the company. Instead the average rating received for his small department was now in the "satisfied" range. While Tom knew that he was still not at the level of "delighting and amazing" customers, he felt that the latest survey results provided some vindication and verification of the actions that Rick and Harry were taking.

When he felt that he was finally ready with his plans, Tom called both men into work early one morning. He began the session by having all three of them *recite in unison the mission and mission task list* that they had developed so long ago. When they were done, Tom invited them to "dig in" to the food that he had brought specially for the meeting…coffee and chocolate glazed donuts for Harry…coffee and two pineapple danishes for Rick. Because Tom had a tendency to over-order, Harry nicknamed these gatherings as 'Tom's Breakfast Beefings.' But, Harry's label also bespoke the real purpose of the gathering…to discuss something that was on Tom's mind.

After some light conversation around current events, Harry resorted to his new "stage voice" and crooned, "So, Tom, now that you got us all buttered-up, what did you really bring us in for?"

Everyone chuckled.

"Well," began Tom, "let me say, first of all, that I'm really pleased with all of the hard work that you guys have been putting into the changes that we've been trying to institute. I've seen some real progress.... particularly in the way that you seem to be consistently using the greetings and expressions that we developed for our callers. The good news is that it looks like we're finally starting to see some 'pay-off' in terms of our customers' reaction to your efforts." Tom then told them about the latest customer satisfaction survey results. He concluded by offering them his own personal "congratulations!"

"Thank you for telling us that, Tom," Harry grinned.

"You're welcome, Harry," Tom replied. "But as you might suspect, we still have a lot of work to do in terms of 'delighting and amazing' our customers...which is the other reason that I brought you in this morning. I need to find out something." Tom paused. "Tell me straight up...right now, apart from the recent customer survey, do either of you have any idea as to how well or poorly you are performing in terms of the goals on the mission task list?"

"I don't know what you mean," Rick replied.

"Well, for instance, do you have any idea as to how well you are doing with respect to your goal of answering the phone within two rings?"

"I don't know," stammered Harry. "Maybe ninety percent."

"I would guess about the same." Rick responded.

Tom thought to himself, "Once again, the wise old man was right. They think that they're doing a pretty good job."

He then said to them, "Well, I'm sorry to have to tell you but I think that we have a bit of a problem here because that's not the impression that I've been getting. You see, I've been giving a lot of thought, these past few days, to the way that I've been monitoring you guys and the way that I've been giving you feedback. And I have come to the conclusion that it's been much too erratic and inconsistent....that the method I've used really doesn't show me...or you, for that matter...whether you are improving or getting into difficulty… and it doesn't allow me to see all the times when you've done something right."

"I'll agree with that," Rick remarked.

"So I've been doing some research and investigating the availability of some of our company's resources…particularly from the IT department. It turns out that they can actually set up the company computer to count the number of times the switchboard phone rings before it gets answered as well as the number of seconds that a caller is put on hold. The IT department can then generate for each of you a report at the end of every day indicating the number of times that you answered calls on the first ring, the second ring, the third ring, or four or more rings. The report will also tell you the average number of rings and the average number of seconds that a caller was kept on hold. That way, if we manage to answer the phones quickly but do so only at the cost of keeping our callers on hold too long, we'll know that we either need more staff or need to relax our two-ring policy."

"That's fantastic," Harry exclaimed. Rick's face grew solemn.

"The best part though," Tom continued, "is that with this system, it is ***totally objective and you*** *can now keep track yourself of how well you are doing over time.* The IT department can generate additional reports showing how quickly the phones are being answered on a daily, weekly, monthly basis. You can then *use this information to monitor your own progress and see where any adjustments need to be made…if any*….So, what do you think?"

"I love it," said Harry. "What do you think, Rick?"

"Well, if you want my honest opinion, Tom, it seems to me that we now have Big Brother watching us."

"I suppose that's one way of looking at it, Rick," replied Tom. "But there's another way as well. It's that we go back to my old method of monitoring performance which you just indicated that you didn't like either… But, look, I'm open to suggestions. If you don't like the method that I'm proposing and can offer a better solution, then I am willing to hear about it and even to try it.….So tell me what you would propose instead?"

After a few moments of uncomfortable silence, Rick responded glumly, "Well, I guess we could try it your way to see how things go."

"That's the spirit Rick" Tom said enthusiastically. "But now comes the harder part. I still haven't been able to figure out a good system to monitor and count the number of times that you guys say a caller's name. I have some ideas but I'd sure love to hear how you both think that we should go about doing this. So, let's try to figure this one out together....okay?...just like we did when we created the mission critical task list."

"Okay, Tom," said Harry using his 'stage voice' again.

Tom then handed each man a small pad of lined paper and asked them to write down all of the ideas that they might have to construct such a measurement system. After a very short while, the three men had developed a system in which it was agreed that, Tom would:

- Listen in and record their phone calls for five minutes each day;
- Count the number of times that a customer's name was mentioned during the calls;
- Evaluate their tone of voice quality on a scale of one to ten; and
- Prepare a weekly and monthly report showing the average, minimum and maximum number of times that each operator said a caller's name as well as the average voice tone quality rating.

It was also agreed that Tom would let either man listen to the tapes whenever they wanted to verify the 'caller name count' that he had recorded for them.

Tom then asked: "Do both of you think that this is a fair way of evaluating your performance?"

"Completely" said Harry. "Not only is it fair, it's also consistent, regular and allows us to track our performance over time to see how we are doing." Rick, though, remained silent and only nodded his head.

"Well, then, let's see how it goes."

As it was time to open up the switchboard, Harry grabbed the remaining plate of food and both operators hurried towards their respective stations.

Over the next several weeks, Tom followed through on the arrangements that he had made with Rick and Harry for measuring their performance and providing them with regular and consistent feedback. As he had originally suspected, the first reports from the IT department showed that neither Rick nor Harry were answering the phone anywhere near the levels that they had predicted. Harry, though, was proving to be the better performer. The reports showed that he was, on average, answering the phone within two (or less) rings about seventy five percent of the time. On the other hand, Rick's score was, according to Tom, an "abysmal" sixty-four percent.

But the reports seemed to have their effect, just as the wise old man had predicted – at least insofar as Harry's performance was concerned. During the following three weeks, Harry's daily "two ring" percentage score increased to ninety-one percent and then appeared to "plateau". Rick's performance, on the other hand, stayed about the same - showing modest gains one week, only to be lost in the following measurement period.

The results concerning each man's performance in terms of saying a caller's name also proved to be not much different. When Harry first learned about his initial score (an average of three times per call), he became extremely motivated to, as he liked to put it, "beat his old record". Because of this, he managed to achieve a level of performance in which he was saying a caller's name an average of seven times. He also held the record for saying a caller's name the most number of times at fourteen. While Rick appeared to be trying to comply with this mission task, his efforts were, nonetheless, significantly below that of Harry's.

The area that proved to be Rick's nemesis, though, was on the ratings he received for 'voice quality'. Harry remained true to his original voice training lessons and consistently applied the 'silky smooth' tones that he had learned to each and every call. It was becoming blatantly obvious, however, that Rick was just simply refusing to even try.

"It's just not me," he told Tom one afternoon as the latter was handing out the weekly performance results.

"I know it's not you, Rick," said Tom. "But, it's what you and Harry both agreed to do…right?…and it also seems to be something that the customer appears to like….just ask Harry."

"I know that …but, I still feel uncomfortable with doing it"

"I see," Tom replied. "But, surely you know by now why we need to be doing this…right?"

"Yes, Tom," said Rick "to delight and amaze our customers in everything we do... but I just don't like doing it, okay."

"No Rick, it's not okay," replied Tom with a hint of impatience in his voice. "There are lots of things that we don't like to do in life but still have to do them anyway. So, think of this as one of those things." Tom's voice then became almost pleading, "Look Rick, I really need you to try and get better at this. Do you want me to send you to the speech therapist again...for some refresher training?"

"No...I know how to do it. I just have a problem getting my mind around doing it."

"Well, then," said Tom, "please know that I really need you to do it. Harry's been able to. So, it looks bad on you if you don't as well. So, Rick, please try...if not for yourself, then for me. I know you can do it if you really care."

But, things did not get much better.

It was then that Tom remembered the rest of the advice that the wise old man had given him – to create personal consequences for Rick and Harry for doing what they needed to do. To this end, he thought of several courses of action. To get additional effort out of both men, Tom announced that he was going to plot and publicly post their "combined" average score for the number of 'rings' on the wall beside their stations. That way, everyone passing their work area could see the degree to which their department was contributing to the company mission and achieving the service standard that they had set for themselves. Because Harry would not want to have his score dragged down by Rick, Tom believed that with this approach, he could enlist Harry's support in helping to motivate Rick.

Tom also announced that he would, at the end of each month, declare in the company newsletter, the name of the operator who scored the highest in terms of repeating a caller's name. Tom even bought a small trophy, which he hoped would rotate between the two men, as a symbol of their friendly rivalry.

Finally, Tom thought that he should speak to Rick specifically about his voice quality problem once more. As he did so, Tom also informed Rick that he would be revising his performance evaluation criteria to take Rick's voice quality score into account as part of his overall annual performance evaluation.

What happened next both amazed and depressed Tom.

Harry responded immediately to the challenges. So much so that he drove his performance score for answering the phone to record levels. He even managed to exceed the standard of two rings – which caused Tom to remark that "sooner or later Harry was going to start answering the phone before it even rang". But there was a down side to the success. Harry started to become much more antagonistic towards Rick – whom he felt was not trying hard enough. "He's making the both of us look bad" Harry told Tom one day on his break.

Similarly, Harry's performance in terms of saying a caller's name defied all expectations. So much so, that it was becoming obvious by the third month that only Harry would ever be the possessor of the trophy. Rick's view, however, was now becoming characteristic. He said that he simply didn't care about such "baubles" - as he put it.

While Tom was delighted with the progress that he had made in helping Harry finally do what the company needed him to do, he was also at odds with Rick's response to all of Tom's efforts. "I've done everything that the wise old man told me to do," he thought to himself, "Yet, I've only managed to succeed with Harry and not with Rick." He could not explain the differences in outcomes that he had achieved. Tom, therefore, promised himself that he would take the next available opportunity to see

Fred and to find out what additional wisdom the wise old man might have for him this time…

Fred's Final Lesson

As Tom explained the situation to the wise old man, Fred listened patiently. When Tom was finished the wise old man repeated his usual litany of questions to him. Only this time the focus was exclusively on Rick.

"Does he *know what to do*?" came Fred's traditional opening volley.

"Of course he does," shot back Tom. "Rick can recite the mission and mission task list flawlessly."

"And does he *know why he should do what you want him to do*?" came the second round.

"Without question. I've asked him to tell me *'the why'* dozens of times. He knows *'the why'*," said Tom with a hint of anger growing in his voice.

"And, does he *know how to do it*?" fired back Fred.

"Yes, he most certainly does," answered Tom. "Now, look here Fred…"

Fred, however, seemed to not even notice Tom's festering annoyance. "And does he *know that he should care* about doing what you need him to do?"

"Indubitably!" replied Tom, almost shouting now. "Fred, listen to everything that I've just told you. I've recounted for you all the things that I've done to try and make Rick feel that he should care and still, I'm not getting the behaviors that Rick needs to be doing. What have I done wrong?" Tom's anger was melting into exasperation.

"Well, my clever young man," came Fred's laconic response, "The answer to your question is simple. It's that you haven't done anything wrong. The problem now no longer lies with you to solve...the problem lies with Rick himself...and, it appears that *he just doesn't get it*!"

"What do you mean 'he just doesn't get it'?" asked Tom somewhat confused at Fred's cryptic words.

"I mean that Rick's personal value system and attitudes appear to be so damaged or corrupted that despite your best efforts to show him *'the what', 'the why', 'the how'* and *'to care'*, he is prepared to dig in his heels and defy your best attempts to help rehabilitate him...His poor values and attitudes also appear to be so entrenched that it might take you many more months - and maybe even years - to try and reverse them...and unfortunately for Rick, you probably don't have that amount of time to devote to him...or do you?

"Not really, Fred," replied Tom.

"Well then, you should probably have a pretty good idea as to what it is that you have to do with him. You see, Tom, the world is full of people like Rick. Your challenge as a leader, therefore, is to avoid – or get rid of – all of 'the Ricks' that you encounter and to find, keep and motivate as many of 'the Harrys' as you can."

Tom looked dejected.

"What's wrong, Tom?"

"It's just that I feel bad about Rick. That somehow I failed him."

"Tom, you didn't fail Rick. He failed himself." Fred took a deep breath and continued, "Tom, you're a talented young leader… and I admire you greatly. But, because of your inexperience, you can't ever allow yourself to forget the most important leadership principle."

"The most important leadership principle?…What's that?" asked Tom.

"It's that when subordinates are not doing what it is that the company needs them to do, *great leaders always blame themselves first*. They say to themselves: 'this problem is my problem…now what can I do about it?' When it comes to difficult subordinates, leaders ask themselves, *"Do they know what to do?"*, *"Do they know why they should be doing it?"*, *"Do they know how to do it?"* and *"Do they know that they should care?"*…and if they can answer "yes" to all four of those questions, then great leaders accept the fact that somehow 'a Rick' made it into their ranks…someone who just doesn't get it… and only then do they not blame themselves first anymore…unless of course they hired 'the Rick' in the first place…which then might mean they have a problem with the way they recruit people. So, go deal with 'your Rick', Tom, and start looking for another 'Harry'. Do you see what I'm saying?"

"I think so," replied Tom.

"Good… then go forth and prosper, Tom…and now get the heck out of here because I have a lot of work to do."

Tom rose from the chair in which he was sitting and thanked Fred profusely for all of his patience and coaching. Tom sensed somewhat wistfully, though, that his days of running to see the wise old man were at an end….that Fred had taught him the most important leadership principle well…. and that now all he had to do was practice it…over and over and over.

He promised himself that he would not disappoint his old mentor and that he would master the ways of leadership as Fred had helped him to learn.

When Tom returned to his office he summarized what Fred had taught him as follows:

The 'Don't Know' Theory of Leadership

There are only five reasons why employees might not do what you need them to do…

It's because they…

i)   Don't know WHAT to do.

ii)   Don't know WHY they should do it.

iii)   Don't know HOW to do it.

iv)   Don't know that they should CARE.

v)   Don't GET IT.

A good leader makes sure that an employee knows the first four things before he concludes that the employee 'doesn't get it'.

A great leader always blames himself first.

Epilogue

The next day Tom asked Rick to see him after work. The two men had an open and honest conversation about what Tom needed Rick to do and what Rick was prepared to give. In light of everything that he had learned the past few months from Fred, it came as no surprise when Rick stated that he was very unhappy with his current job and that he wanted a change. Tom promised to help Rick find another position that was more to his liking and attitude. Rick thanked Tom with a sincerity that the clever young man had never seen before.

Both men went home that evening feeling good about themselves.

****

Two years passed. Fred retired. Harry married one of the callers. And Tom got his second promotion – this time a big one. By now, though,Tom had earned quite a reputation for himself in the organization. He was known as someone who knew how to get the job done....who knew how to make the company's mission matter and to make it come alive. His little department had even managed to win the company's 'customer satisfaction award'. Everyone called him a natural born leader.

Then, one day, as he was beginning to settle into his new office, a knock came at the door. It was Sandra Rosen. She had just been given responsibility for managing a small but new department of four people. It was her first leadership assignment and Tom thought of her as a clever young woman. She said:

"Can you spare me a few moments, Tom?"

"Sure," came Tom's reply. "What can I do for you?"

"Well," she began "I've got this new assignment with some new subordinates who are not doing what the company needs them to do and I was wondering if you could give me some advice on how I might deal with them?"

"I see," said the now wise, but still **quite** young, Tom. "I'll certainly try. So, tell me, Sandra, do they know what to do?..."

THE END

Promotional Buttons

Dr. Christopher Kenneth Bart
North America's leading mission and vision expert.

Dr. Christopher Bart is North America's leading expert on helping organizations develop *mission and vision statements* that get results. He has published over 50 articles, cases and reviews and he has a unique expertise in helping firms organize their internal structure to better achieve their mission.

Dr. Bart is currently a principal with **Corporate Missions Inc.** (www.corporatemissionsinc.com) and a **Professor of Business Administration at the Michael G. DeGroote School of Business, McMaster University**, Hamilton, Ontario. In 1993, he helped found the Management of Innovation & New Technology Research Centre (MINT~RC) at McMaster and was named its first Director. In 1994, he conceived and created the Innovation Management Network - a world-wide association of academics and practitioners who communicate and collaborate on matters of innovation and new technology management through the Internet.

A highly regarded lecturer, Dr. Bart has been named both "Outstanding Undergraduate Business Professor" (1982 and 1997) and "MBA Professor of the Year" (1984, 1989 and 1991). In 1995, he received McMaster's highest teaching award: The President's Award for Teaching Excellence.

Over the years, Dr. Bart has been invited to lecture at numerous prestigious institutions throughout the world including:

The University Cape Town (S.A.), Cranfield Institute of Technology (U.K.), Monash University (Aus.), The Czech Management Centre, and Fudan University (China). He has also received many academic awards and honours.

Among his other qualifications, Dr. Bart is a Chartered Accountant. He is a past Director of the Planning Executives Institute and has been a member of numerous company Boards of Directors and professional organizations. He is listed in Canadian WHO'S WHO.

To contact Dr Bart:

Phone: 905 - 308 - 8455
Fax: 905 - 308-8284
e-mail: chrisbart@corporatemissionsinc.com